Adventures of a First Year Teacher
in a Third World Country

ADVENTURES OF A
FIRST YEAR TEACHER
IN A
THIRD WORLD COUNTRY

DON HAYES

iUniverse, Inc.
Bloomington

**Adventures of a First Year Teacher
in a Third World Country**

iUniverse books may be ordered through booksellers or by contacting:

iUniverse
1663 Liberty Drive
Bloomington, IN 47403
www.iuniverse.com
1-800-Authors (1-800-288-4677)

ISBN: 978-1-4502-7391-6 (sc)
ISBN: 978-1-4502-7392-3 (ebk)

Printed in the United States of America

iUniverse rev. date: 11/19/2010

CONTENTS

Preface

It has been almost thirty years since I lived in Bolivia. Santa Cruz has quadrupled in size since then, and the house where I lived (if it still exists), instead of being on the edge of the Amazon jungle, is actually closer to the center of town than the jungle! The city did not continue to expand in concentric rings, the fourth ring being the outermost. Bolivia is now a democracy and I'm sure it's standard of living is much higher, but it's real wealth is its people, and I'm sure they are still as friendly as ever.

I would like to thank Kate Lacy for all of her help in making me a better writer. I would also like to thank my wife Linda for proofreading my work and encouraging me.

Fayetteville, Arkansas   D.H.
July 2010

To my friends and family,
I hope you find this entertaining.

WELCOME TO BOLIVIA

As the airplane banked, I could see the city of La Paz in the bowl-shaped valley below. Although the sun would soon be up, lights could still be seen twinkling in the city. I was filled with a mixture of excitement and apprehension as we descended onto the runway of "El Alto", the highest commercial airport in the world.

Walking down the steps and onto the airport tarmac, I began to feel lightheaded, and it was not from the excitement or lack of sleep. At over 3900 meters, "El Alto" is more than twice as high as Denver and has about one half the available oxygen as New York or San Francisco. While I was standing in the brisk morning air, I saw an amazing sight in the distance. It was a massive, snow-covered mountain, a sentinel rising thousands of meters above the surrounding plains. Its name: Illimani. I've seen the Rockies and the Alps, but I have never seen anything to compare with the grandeur of the Andes.

We walked over to a table that had been set up on the asphalt near the terminal building, and the armed guards began to check our passports. Those of us who were going on to Santa Cruz would stay out here and board another airplane. They asked for my baggage claim tickets so they could make sure my bags would be safely transferred to the Santa Cruz plane. Little did I know that I was never to see those ticket stubs again. We stood in the chilly morning air waiting for our plane. Except for the airport buildings and the aircraft parked on the flight line, there wasn't much to see. After about thirty minutes, we boarded our plane and had an uneventful flight to the tropical lowlands of Santa Cruz.

Santa Cruz is as different from La Paz as Miami is from Minneapolis. The cool, crisp air of the Altiplano was replaced by the hot, humid air of the tropics. The lush vegetation that surrounded the airport was punctuated with tall palm trees. As we walked from the airplane to the terminal building, I could feel the oppressive heat, even though it was only nine in the morning.

Once inside, I looked for the people who were supposed to meet me, but there was no one holding a sign with my name on it. In fact, there wasn't even anyone there that looked like a North American. I was able to get checked through customs, but since I didn't have my baggage claim tickets, they wouldn't let me have my bags.

I sat on a bench in the airport terminal staring through the terminal entrance with a mixture of anger and disappointment. I couldn't believe that they did this to me. They gave me a job, asked me to fly down to Bolivia, said that they'd meet me at the airport, and then didn't show up. Now I'm in a foreign country, can hardly speak the language, don't know anybody, and to top it all off, can't even get my baggage.

Outside, I could see the long, naked trunks of the palm trees. They cast little shadow from the high tropical sun. The tree tops formed pools of shade around the base of each tree. The avenue leading from the airport was lined with flowering shrubs, and the grass was closely clipped. It was a picture postcard.

A movement pulled my gaze into the terminal. A stocky Indian in dingy clothes was loaded down with suitcases and packages. Behind him, at a proper distance, were the owners of those packages. They were a well-dressed couple from their neat hair to their polished shoes. There was a little girl to my right, her tiny fist clenching her mother's dress, staring at me. She had large, dark eyes and a runny nose. Across the room, stood a soldier in a dark green uniform. The red loops on the shoulder straps were held in place with brass buttons, and a gold and red braid looped down from his right shoulder. His garrison cap had a highly polished black visor pulled down low over his eyes. A sub-machine gun hung from a leather strap on his back. There was no doubt who was in control of this building.

There was no air conditioning, so the doors to the outside were open. The air was thick with smells – grease from the café upstairs, sweat from the people around me, the kerosene smell of the jet fuel that wafted in from the flight line. My North American nose, used to air that has been filtered, dehumidified, sanitized, and sanctified, was particularly sensitive to these smells.

Then I noticed that someone was walking toward me. He had a nice face, a pleasant smile, and was wearing jeans. "Hi, I'm Larry Cooper, the principal. Are you the new science teacher?"

"Yes I am."

"Sorry I'm late, but the school van wouldn't start. Welcome to Bolivia."

SANTA CRUZ

⌒⁓

Larry had to do a little talking and a little bribing, but he was able to get my bags out of the holding area successfully. As we walked out of the airport terminal, Larry told me that I was one of the first teachers to arrive in Santa Cruz for the new school year and the others would be arriving later in the week.

The heat of the tropics beat down on us as we approached the school vehicle: an old, beat-up, orange minivan with the words *Escuela Cooperativa de Santa Cruz* (Santa Cruz Cooperative School) painted on the side with black letters. We threw the bags in the back, climbed in, and headed down the boulevard that lead away from the airport.

As we drove, I looked in wonder at the incredible beauty that was everywhere. There were some trees covered with yellow flowers, others had deep purple blossoms. Some of the shrubs lining the streets were spherical, others rectangular, some were not pruned at all. They were a collection of hues: emerald, sage, lime, and jade. These provided soothing shade and a contrast to the brilliant blue sky. At the intersections with other main streets, there were traffic circles with fountains spouting jets of water in displays of liquid fireworks. Many of these were planted with flowers so vivid in color they seemed iridescent.

The streets were paved with hexagonal stone blocks about ten centimeters thick and half a meter across. They were not held together with with cement or asphalt but placed tightly against one another. This caused the surface to be somewhat uneven in places and made it feel like driving on gentle ocean swells. The houses were all set back from the avenue with their front lawns obscured from view by stone or brick walls. This gave the illusion of driving down a long, wide hallway with rapidly changing walls and a rough, green ceiling.

The walls were all topped with jagged, broken glass which had been set in concrete. This was done to discourage thieves from climbing the walls to rob the houses. Santa Cruz had problems with crimes against property. Burglary was very common in Santa Cruz, and there were teachers who had their homes broken into more than once during the year I was there. However, crimes against people were very rare. During the time I was in Santa Cruz, there were no instances of sexual assault and only one murder, and this was in a city twice the size of Little Rock! A person felt safe anywhere in Santa Cruz.

Larry slowed the van, and we turned into the entrance of a driveway. The wrought iron gate prevented us from pulling entirely off the street, so the back of the van stuck out into the roadway. Larry wasn't worried though, it was Sunday, and there wasn't much traffic.

"Is this your house?" I asked, as Larry got out of the van to open the gate.

"No this is the Nelsons' house. They arrived last night, and I wanted to check on them. This will give you the chance to meet a couple of the other teachers, then we'll go. You're not in a hurry, are you?"

"No, that's fine. I don't have anything else to do."

The driveway consisted of two concrete strips that the tires drove on which led up to the house. Along the drive were strange green plants and flowers. The lawn was nicely trimmed, and a wide variety of shrubs broke up the monotony of the gray wall that surrounded the house and lawn. Up near the house were large dark green mango trees with thick, shiny leaves. After walking back to the street to close the driveway gate, we walked up to the front door and knocked.

I could hear loud music coming from inside, then footsteps, and finally the door swung open. A lank young man with a thick, brown beard squinted as he looked out into the bright daylight. Recognition spread across his face, and he smiled, "Larry!"

"Dennis!"

"Come on in. Do you want a beer?"

"Sure. This is Don Hayes, our new science teacher. He just arrived from the States."

"Hi, Don. Want a beer?"

"Sure."

It was dark and cool inside the house. Two large speakers were blaring out The Grateful Dead, and empty beer bottles were scattered around the room. An ashtray was brimming with butts. Someone was having a good time. A moment later his wife, Ginny, came into the living room. She had a nice smile and a glass of wine in her hand. Larry, Dennis, and Ginny spent about half an hour catching up on news. Then Larry and I left.

As we were heading out toward his house, Larry explained that Santa Cruz was laid out in concentric rings. As we passed the third ring, there was a lot of open land on both sides of the highway. I could see the jungle beyond the fields and the Andes Mountains in the distance.

We made a right-hand turn onto a sandy road. The sand was packed, so that we were able to drive on it without sinking. Up ahead on the right, about two blocks from the highway, was the school, and a half block beyond that was Larry's house. We pulled into the driveway.

"My wife is in Chile visiting her parents, so you can spend the night here, and then tomorrow we'll see if we can find you a place to live."

GOLPE!

I woke up early, my first full day in Santa Cruz, filled with a sense wonder and excitement. Here I was in a new country with a new job - a whole new world. Larry was already up and listening to the radio.

"Good morning, Larry."

"'Morning, Don. We're having a revolution."

A lot of times when I first get up, my mind is not functioning at full capacity, and I don't hear things quite as clearly as I should. Not wanting to appear stupid, I simply repeated, "A revolution?"

"Yes, General Salazar has taken Santa Cruz and is moving on La Paz. The air force is supporting him. All citizens are to remain in their homes until further notice."

Great! I haven't even been in the country twenty-four hours, and already we have a revolution. "What do we do?" I asked.

"Not much. We'll drink some beer, play a little *cacho,* and maybe later on walk over to the school."

He seemed to be taking this rather well. And what was this business about walking over to the school, I thought we had been ordered to stay indoors. One of us was not in touch with reality, and what worried me, I wasn't sure which one.

This is a good time to talk about one of Bolivia's richest traditions: the *golpe* or revolution. The word *golpe* means strike or blow (against the government). Since its independence in 1825, Bolivia has had some 170 revolutions. This figures out to about one a year. Here is how the system works: a general will seize power, help himself to the country's wealth, and when the next revolution comes along, retire quite comfortably. There is rarely any bloodshed, in fact, the ousted general is usually not even imprisoned. When a general has been in power long enough, he usually will not try to prevent another one from taking over. It's nice that the generals share.

The Bolivian people understand the system very well, perhaps even better than the generals. During the revolution, they stay away from military targets such as airports, power plants, and radio stations and off the main streets. Notice that I said main streets: usually after the first four to six hours, people would travel the back streets to do shopping and take care of their daily business. They just need to make sure they are in small enough groups so they wouldn't be considered counter-revolutionary. I saw a man pushing his bicycle along the side of the road with two bags of groceries tied onto the back of his bike just hours after the revolution had begun. He didn't seem to have a care in the world.

To the Bolivians, the endless stream of generals is viewed with a sense of humor. There is even a perverse sense of pride in the fact that Bolivia holds the record for the most governments since independence. It should be noted that not all of the leaders of Bolivia are without compassion for the poor. Martín Banzer, for example, was in power for seven years and had many schools, hospitals, and parks built. There were many working people who would like to see him back in power.

After Larry explained the realities of revolution to me, I was much more relaxed. We spent most of the time around the house. We did some repairs around the house, played some *cacho,* and walked over to the school to get some work done. The school was only a block from Larry's house, and it was on a side street, so we couldn't be seen by the soldiers patrolling the main highway.

One of the most unusual things we did was to call our families back in the States to let them know we were safe. If I were conducting a revolution, one of the first things I would do would be to seize control of all the communication centers, but what do I know, I'm not a general!

The revolution lasted five days. During that time, no new teachers were able to arrive, and Larry was able to get a lot done to get the school ready for opening. As a first-year science teacher, I made use of the time to inventory all of the science equipment and write lesson plans for the first week. Since I taught all of the high school science classes, it took me about two and a half days to inventory all of the equipment. The revolution caused the school to open a week late, but that didn't cause much inconvenience since we had revolution days built into our school calendar just like many schools in the States have snow days built into their schedules.

I spent a very productive and relaxing week during the revolution. A few times we walked up to the *tienda*, or local grocery store, to buy beer, potatoes, and eggs. It was then that I began to appreciate the incredible beauty of the area around Santa Cruz and the warmth of the Bolivian people.

WE REALLY NEED TO DESTROY THIS SODIUM

⚜

The school was down the road about a half a kilometer off the *Carretera Cochabamba* (Cochabamba Highway). The school was situated at the corner of two streets, with the front along one street, and the bus area, with two large school buses, along the other. Off to the right of the entryway to the main school area was a round building that housed the kindergarten through second grade.

The main part of the school was made up of four one story buildings, each about forty meters in length. These formed a square in the center with open walkways. Inside the square was a luscious, cool grassy area shaded by two large trees. A sidewalk ran around three sides of this square. The sidewalk was covered by a metal overhang which kept the students dry from the frequent tropical downpours. There were shrubs along the third side covered with small lavender and white flowers. Small, red birds not much larger than hummingbirds, would flit among the shrubs as the air sparkled with the calls of tropical birds. The classrooms opened onto this paradise.

My classroom was next to the principal's office. The key to the classroom was a large, old-fashioned key like those seen on a jailer's key ring. The science room was twice the size of a regular classroom, with student and teacher desks in the front half of the classroom. An ancient slate blackboard was on the front wall, and the lab area was in the back. Counters ran down both sides of the room, with storage cabinets underneath. A glass covered cabinet loaded with biology models hung on the back wall. A standard school clock hung above the cabinet. It was an American clock, and when it ran on the fifty cycle current of Bolivia, the hands only moved fifty minutes an hour. It was an endless source of amusement for my students, but it did give the correct time every three days!

The first task facing me was to find out how much equipment I had. I pulled all of the equipment from the cabinets and divided it up into five categories: physics, chemistry, biology, geology, and unknown. There was a fair amount of equipment, and overall, it was in pretty good condition. Someone must have been given a special bargain in glassware, because there was enough glassware to teach chemistry for fifty years! I labeled the boxes by category and stored the equipment on the shelves.

Next I tackled the supplies, most of which chemicals. The labels on some of the containers were missing or decomposed so badly that they could not be read. These, along with broken glass, I set aside in a box to be disposed of later. The rest of the chemicals had been purchased locally or shipped down from the States. Since most scientific and mathematical terms from the last two hundred years are similar in most languages, it was easy to determine what the chemicals were, even those with labels in Spanish.

Everything went along smoothly until I opened the cabinet under the sink. There, in old rusted cans, was about half a kilogram of sodium! Any first-year chemistry student will tell you that sodium is a highly reactive metal. So reactive that it will explode when it comes into contact with water. And here it was being stored in rusty cans, under a leaky sink, surrounded by glass containers of hydrochloric and sulfuric acid. It was a disaster waiting to happen. That much sodium would have destroyed the back of the lab, throwing burning acid and shards of glass into a classroom full of students. I put on rubber gloves and very carefully moved the cans from under the sink to a table in the center of the room. I locked the classroom, found Larry, and told him that we needed to destroy about three-fourths of the sodium.

There are all sorts of sayings about how good lies within evil and victory within defeat: the Silver Lining Theory. Such was the case with this sodium. When handled correctly, sodium is no more dangerous than marshmallows (except you can't eat sodium). I told

Larry that he should observe me while I destroyed the sodium.

About four in the afternoon, we left the school and went to Larry's back yard where I set up a small tub of water and an old wooden crate that I used as a cutting table. We put two chairs about five meters away from the tub, popped open a couple of bottles of beer, and proceeded to enjoy life. I would carefully cut off a piece of sodium about the size of a marble and toss it into the tub of water. It would explode, sending a shower of sparks and water into the air. We would laugh and repeat the procedure.

After a while, the continued use of the water would reduce its ability to react violently with the sodium, so I would pour fresh water into the tub and continue. We spent a very relaxing afternoon under the tropical skies destroying sodium and drinking beer. Teaching was so much fun, and I hadn't even seen my first student!

BEYOND THE FOURTH RING

⌒⫞⌒

As the revolution was winding down, things were returning to normal in Santa Cruz. Flights from Miami were to resume tomorrow, and the rest of the faculty would be arriving soon. Although teachers usually lived together in twos or threes, so they could pool their housing allowance money and get a nicer place, I had already been in Bolivia for a week and didn't want to wait two or three more days to find a place to live. Larry had agreed to take me around Santa Cruz in the school van and help translate for me.

As we drove around the city, we saw tanks at some of the intersections and armed soldiers everywhere. I soon found out why so many teachers lived together: the housing allowance for a single teacher would pay for little more than a hut with broken-down furniture. I was appalled. Larry suggested I might do better if I looked at some places farther from the center of town. If you look at a map of the city of Santa Cruz, the center of town is like the bullseye of a large target. Santa Cruz is laid out in concentric rings, each ring one kilometer farther out than the preceding one. Although the inner rings were magnificent boulevards, the fourth (and outermost) ring was little more than a wide path hacked out of the Amazon jungle.

Eventually I found a nice place two blocks beyond the fourth ring on a dirt road. It was about one kilometer from the school, so it was within walking distance. Although I was on the fringe of the city, I was only a block south of the *Carretera Cochabamba*, and the buses ran out to the fourth ring, so it was easy to go into town.

At one time my house had been used as a maid's quarters. It was small, about sixty square meters, and clean. It had two bedrooms (one was so small it had room for a twin bed and nothing else), a bathroom, kitchen, and dining room/living room combination. The bathroom and kitchen were so small I could touch opposite walls at the same time. Every room had windows with screens so they could be opened to let in the fresh air. This was important because the house had no heat or air conditioning (this was common in all but the most expensive homes and businesses). All the floors and the sidewalk out front were covered with large red tiles. Behind the building was a large sink with a faucet where I could do my laundry.

The cottage was modestly furnished with a bed, gas stove, refrigerator, reading chair, and dining room table with three chairs. In addition to that, I was lucky enough to have a telephone, which meant I wouldn't have to wait months to have one installed. I had brought all my kitchen utensils, books, bedding, radio and tape player, and a 220-volt converter from the States, so I was quite comfortable.

My cottage was on the same land as my landlord's house. About thirty meters behind behind my dwelling was a large pit my landlord had dug to throw trash in. Over the years, he had cleared out enough of the jungle for his house, two outbuildings, and about four hundred fruit trees. One of the benefits of renting from him was that I could pick the fruit from any of the fruit trees in the orchard. There were grapefruit, orange, lemon, avocado, banana, mango, and papaya trees, so I had a large variety of fresh fruit to choose from. I still recall, with great pleasure, going out to pick a grapefruit for breakfast or an avocado for lunch.

I bought a tank of propane gas for my kitchen stove from my landlord (it cost about four dollars and would last one or two weeks). Then I went across the highway to a *tienda* where I bought some potatoes, onions, beer, toilet paper, bread, and instant coffee. I cooked my first meal in my new home, and after supper, I took a little walk to check out my new surroundings.

The warm sand on the street gave way under my feet and slowed my progress, but it felt good, and I was in no hurry. Along the street, behind walls, were beautiful houses with stunning flowering trees: orange and lavender and yellow. A wide variety of wild flowers grew along both sides of the street, a flock of parrots flew overhead, and dazzling butterflies danced in the evening breeze. The tropical evening surrounded my body and filled me with a sense of tranquility.

Night was beginning to fall, so I walked back to the house. I placed a chair outside my front door, opened a bottle of beer, and breathed in the night. The air was heavily scented with jasmine, and the high-pitched whine of the cicadas came from every direction. In the distance, a bird let out a sorrowful call. The night air was warm and soft on my skin. Everything conspired to relax me. This was heaven.

THE TIENDA

If you were to examine how I spent my time while living in Santa Cruz, you would find that most of the time I was at home or at school. Much of the remaining time I would be at the local *tienda*. The *tienda* is a small grocery store, similar to the mom and pop stores so common in the United States during the first half of the twentieth century.

Except for meat, which was purchased at the meat market, you could buy just about anything you needed at the *tienda*. They had eggs, sugar, crackers, cookies, beer, and soft drinks, as well as cans of peaches and sardines, jars of olives, boxes of soup, and other packaged food items. There were bins of potatoes and onions in the back, and on the front wooden counter were bowls with oranges, grapefruit, avocados, and papayas. They also had necessary non-food items such as light bulbs, matches, toilet paper, soap, and mosquito coils.

Tiendas differ from American grocery stores in two important ways. In the first place, they are similar in construction and size to fireworks stands, with three walls and a counter in front. They are square in shape, about six or seven meters on a side. The sun and rain are kept out by a hinged board which hangs above the customers. This board is swung down at night when the shop is locked up. We would stand outside the counter, tell the owner what we wanted, and they would get it for us.

The second difference, and the reason I spent so much time at the *tienda*, was that there were chairs or stools at the counter so a person could sit down, relax, and enjoy a bottle of beer. This is probably a good time to discuss beer drinking in Bolivia. With very few televisions to distract people, there was more time for conversation and social interaction. People, men in particular, would sit for hours drinking and talking. It seemed to be a cultural pastime, one which I embraced wholeheartedly. Since Bolivian beer was served in liter bottles, you had better not be in a hurry. I would sit at the counter or a table under a nearby shade tree and enjoy my bottle of beer in the heat of the tropical day. I would sit for hours and watch the people as they came and went. Some would stop by to buy a few potatoes or a kilo of sugar. Many would be walking or riding bicycles along the fourth ring. My favorites were the occasional ox cart trundling along the dusty road or the family of four riding a motorcycle. Sometimes I would just look at the palm trees standing against the background of a brilliant blue sky as fluffy white clouds drifted lazily over the jungle.

The beer was never cold. The owner would remove the bottle from an ancient cooler that would whine and wheeze and barely keep the beer cooler than the ambient air temperature. It didn't matter which *tienda* you were to visit, they all had whiny, wheezy coolers with warm beer. I don't think there was a cold bottle of beer in the entire country of Bolivia, but that made it all the more exotic. My American taste for cold beer declined, and I soon began to enjoy the fuller, richer taste of warm beer.

Most *tiendas* also had dice and a *cacho* cup that they would be happy to let you use. *Cacho* is an old Incan dice game similar to the game of Yahtzee®. Playing cacho was always a pleasant way to pass the time while sitting around talking with friends. Two rules made the game more fun to play: you had to take a drink anytime you rolled the dice off the table or placed the dice in the cup as you passed it to the next player. The game was so popular in Bolivia that on Friday nights, fifty or more men could be seen sitting in front of bars playing *cacho*.

All *tiendas* were owned and operated by families. Our favorite was Sonya and Roxann's, named after the two sisters that ran it. Both were in their late twenties. Roxann was outgoing and usually out on a date with her boyfriend. Sonya was plump and plain, but she had a heart of gold and one if the nicest smiles I have ever seen. Occasionally their younger brother or sister would run the *tienda*. Marioli was sixteen and was in high school. Pablo was eleven and always seemed to have some ingenious device he made from wires, motors, and batteries.

One of Pablo's most amazing gadgets was a device for the electrolysis of water. He had an electrical cord with the end cut off. The tips of both wires had been stripped of insulation. He then placed two inverted glasses in a pan of water and ran one of the wires into each glass. He plugged this apparatus into an AC/DC converter which he had acquired, and when he plugged this into the wall outlet, bubbles started forming at each electrode: hydrogen at one and oxygen at the other! Pablo also knew how to resurrect house flies. Occasionally, a fly would be found floating in a glass of beer on the counter. The fly would not be moving and would appear to be dead. Pablo would fish it out, place it in an ashtray, and have us put cigarette ashes on it. He would roll the fly in the ashes and gently blow on it. After a few minutes, the fly would move around, start buzzing, and fly away. Pablo was an amazing kid.

We frequented Sonya and Roxann's on such a regular basis that when they saw Larry and me walking down the road, they would have the bottles of beer waiting for us on the counter. We would sit and chat for a while. It was a great way for me to improve my Spanish. They were like family to us, and I suppose we were like family to them. Their father even invited Larry and me to his wife's birthday party. Out of the fifty or so guests at at the party, we were the only *Gringos*. We spent the evening eating, drinking, and listening to music from a local band. The Bolivians liked to have a good time, and they liked to share it with friends.

Without a doubt, some of the most relaxing times of my life were those tropical days sitting in the shade, drinking beer, and enjoying life. It brings to mind a line from the movie "Field of Dreams" that I paraphrase here: "Is this heaven? No, this is Bolivia".

TEACHING AT SCCS

eaching at Santa Cruz Cooperative School was a gratifying experience. The Bolivians valued education. It was the opportunity for the improvement of their children individually and their country collectively. In addition to that, as a private school, any miscreants were given three chances to behave appropriately. After the third infraction, they were expelled, and the school kept their tuition. They were motivated.

Since we were an American school, we had the same schedule as in the States. We went five days a week (as opposed to five and a half), and school was in session from mid August until early June. Since we were south of the equator, local schools went from March to November which was their cool season. As a concession to the local community, we did have four weeks off for Christmas vacation. The high school had seven periods a day. Teachers taught five hours and had two preparation periods. The office and library were the only places in the school that were air conditioned, but the classrooms had ceiling fans, and that was enough to keep us from being uncomfortably hot. There was no heat in the school, which did not pose a problem except when a *surazo* (cold front) blew up from the South Pole. All classes were taught in English with the exception of French and Spanish classes which were taught in Spanish.

Even though we were an American school, most of the students (about seventy percent) were the sons and daughters of wealthy Bolivians. Because of their position, some of the students arrived at school in chauffeur driven cars with armed body guards. A few of my students were children of former Bolivian presidents, and Miss Bolivia was in my physics class! About twenty percent were American and British students whose parents were missionaries or worked in the oil fields in the area. The remaining students were Russian, French, and Chinese who were children of the various consulates and embassies in Santa Cruz.

As teachers, we were treated exceptionally well by the parents. If we were seen walking in town or waiting for a bus, parents would stop their cars and offer us a ride to wherever we needed to go. One time, after I had finished a meal in a restaurant and went to pay, the owner told me that a teacher of his child would never pay in his restaurant. When Linda and I announced our engagement, the former first lady of Bolivia gave a formal tea in our honor.

There were many other acts of kindness shown to us. One of my students invited me to play golf with him at the country club. The faculty was invited to the Chinese consulate for cocktails one afternoon. Another one of my students, the son of Martín Banzar, invited me to spend spring break at his family's hacienda. He assured me that I would not have to spend any time with him. I would stay in my own guest cottage, have access to the tennis courts, and swimming pool, and have servants wait on me all day!

There are two other episodes I would like to relate which illustrate the regard the Bolivian people had for teachers. The first involved one of my students who was having difficulty in chemistry and asked if I would tutor her after school. When she asked how much I charged, I told her I didn't charge my students for help. For weeks we worked after school. Her grade gradually increased until she was one of the top students in my class. One afternoon I returned from checking my mail, expecting her to be waiting for me in the classroom. Instead, on my desk was a thank you note and a very expensive bottle of French cognac! The other, and perhaps more touching, incident involved Dr. Hwang and his wife. Their son and daughter were my students. They had emigrated from China, where he had been a physician. He was unable to acquire a license to practice medicine in Bolivia, so he and his wife opened a restaurant. Near the end of the school year, he invited all of his children's teachers, the high school principal, the school's director, and their spouses to a formal dinner at his restaurant. The dinner was in a private dining room at the restaurant. At each place setting, an individual menu was printed for the six course dinner. Doctor Hwang and his wife served the entire dinner. At the end of the meal, when we thanked him, he said, "Oh, no. Thank you for being my children's teachers". I have never since been treated with such honor and respect.

DINING IN SANTA CRUZ

ℳ

Bolivian cuisine is not an oxymoron! Santa Cruz offered many delicious local and regional dishes. (Anyone who lives in a large American city can sample these by going to a Bolivian or Peruvian restaurant.) While we were in Bolivia, we were warned about eating dairy products or raw vegetables but there were no other restrictions.

There seemed to be an unlimited supply of street vendors selling food in Santa Cruz. We could buy a slab of beef or pork in a roll, popcorn from the *pipoca* boys outside the cinemas, frozen ice pops made from banana or orange, or fried banana chips that had been lightly salted. This last item may sound a little weird, but they were quite tasty. They were made from plantains and did not have the sweetness of the bananas we are more familiar with in the States.

One of my favorite foods was the *salteña*. Although they were primarily sold by vendors, they could also be purchased in some stores. The basic recipe was a pie crust filled with onion, beef, potatoes, *ají*, olives, and various spices. (Some also had egg or raisins added.) These were then baked or fried. They were hand-sized and made a great snack. A close relative was the *empanada* which was about half the size, had no vegetables, except onions, and had cheese inside.

Ají (sometimes called *yaqua*) is the national hot sauce, and it is more fiery than anything I have ever tasted. It is made by crushing hot peppers, including seeds and skin, and mixing them with oil. This ubiquitous condiment is served in a small bowl at virtually every Bolivian meal. Meals in Santa Cruz were very inexpensive, most costing one to three dollars.

Bolivia is noted for its soups and stews. Some of my favorites were *sopa de mani* which is a peanut soup with potatoes and carrots, *chicharrón*: a soup or stew made with fried pork pieces, and *chuňo,* a soup which is with made from dark, freeze-dried potatoes. If I wanted a taste of home, there was a pizza shop located on a side street near a pool parlor. The pizza had a Bolivian twist: they put a couple of fried eggs on top!

One typical *Cruzeňo* food is *surubí. Surubí* is a giant catfish (about 1.7 meters in length and weighing in at 50 kilograms). It is found in the Pirai river, a tributary of the Amazon. This fish is usually served as a steak which has been baked or broiled with a minimum of spices or sauces. It has a texture that is not quite as firm as swordfish and is very tasty. Whenever *surubí* was on the menu, I ordered it! Another dish common in Santa Cruz is beef with a side of rice or fried yucca root. Fried yucca root is almost identical to French fries, being just a bit sweeter. Most of the beef was very lean and a bit tough but very tasty.

One of the best dishes to try in Santa Cruz is *pollo a la brasa*. It is chicken cooked over red-hot coals. Three or four chickens are put on a spit, then about ten of these spits are placed on a motor driven chain which moves the chickens over the coals for hours. The result is some of the best tasting chicken in the world. It is succulent with a hint of smoke flavor from the burning wood coals. One of the most heartbreaking scenes at some of the outdoor restaurants occurred at the end of the meal, when the street urchins would come to the table to get the food scraps before the plates were cleared away.

I have forgotten the names of many of my favorite dining establishments, but here is a list of places I would go and the types of food they offered. There were many Chinese restaurants in Santa Cruz, and they offered a good selection of dishes. Sometimes the ladies who ran the *tiendas* would offer a mixture of meat and rice which they made. There was a juice shop in the downtown area which offered a selection of freshly squeezed strawberry, citrus, watermelon, and papaya juices. Also in the area was an oriental bakery which had rice cakes steamed in banana leaves. The 25 de Febrero offered local dishes at a very reasonable price. For *pollo a la brasa*, Pollo de

Oro and Pollo King Kong were the best. We liked to go to El Presidente which was on the fifth floor of the tallest building in Santa Cruz (it was a six story building). It offered a nice view of the downtown area. Near the airport was a restaurant that offered Brazilian mixed grill. To reach it, we followed a curvy path lined with palm fronds. The El Presidio Café offered coffee, rolls, fruit, sandwiches, and a great view of the square. Finally, there was a large open market that offered grilled meat. Every conceivable part of pigs, cows, and chickens could be purchased from about fifty different vendors.

BUSHMASTERS, WHEEL BUGS,
AND OTHER TERRORS

꙳

When most people think about living in the tropics, they have visions of sitting on a beach, sipping an exotic drink with umbrellas, while off in the distance the native people are happily working in the sun. There are also palm trees, colorful birds, and flowers, lots of flowers. The tropics have a sinister side as well. The year-round warm temperatures provide an environment in which all sorts of insects and diseases thrive. Not only do they thrive, but since there is no cold season, as in the temperate zones, there is no time of the year in which these evil things are killed.

Some of the most interesting insects were the leaf cutter ants (also known as parasol ants). These ants live underground and come out at night to gather leaves which they use indirectly for food. A colony will strip a two story tree bare in a single night. In the evening a medium-sized tree will be in front of your house; in the morning, there won't be a single leaf on it. They cut the leaves into nickel-sized pieces and then carry the pieces over their heads like parasols back to their nest. One night I followed a line of leaf cutters for almost a hundred meters.

Mosquitoes were a problem. I was very lucky to have a complete set of screens on my windows, so they didn't bother me. The next best defense was mosquito netting which was placed in a canopy over the bed. As long as it was tucked in under the mattress, it worked great. Mosquito coils were a poor third choice. They were a piece of punk formed into a coil and would burn four to six hours. We would light the end, and it would smolder and fill the room with a thick smoke which the mosquitoes didn't like. It was not pleasant to breathe the smoke, but it was better than having mosquitoes feasting on your flesh. One night when my coil burned out and I didn't have a replacement, the mosquitoes were biting with such ferocity, I was forced to cover myself with the sheet until morning.

The largest of the dangerous animals is the bushmaster. The bushmaster is a large, poisonous snake native to the American tropics. What makes this snake particularly frightening, is it will deliberately attack humans instead of slithering away. In fact, there are certain times of the year when the laborers around Santa Cruz refuse to work in the fields, even if they are armed with machetes. I am happy to say that I never saw one of these vicious snakes alive.

More frightening than the bushmaster is the wheel bug. The wheel bug is not dangerous in itself, but some of them carry the deadly Chargas disease. There are probably as many stories about Chargas disease as there are people in Bolivia. The most bizarre story I heard was, if you were bitten by the wheel bug, you would keel over from a heart attack in twenty years. I am always skeptical when I hear stories like this, so I started asking people who lived in the area to tell me about this mysterious disease. It turns out the disease is actually caused by microscopic parasites which live in the digestive tract of the wheel bug (a blood-sucking assassin bug *vinchuca*). After a person is bitten, the victim becomes infected. The disease has two stages: first the person becomes sick with flu-like symptoms for a few weeks, then, the muscles in the body slowly deteriorate, until, after twenty years or so the heart is destroyed.

Because of this, we were told always to shake out our shoes before we put them on and never to walk barefooted. One morning, I forgot to do this and put on my shoes without checking them first. I felt a sharp sting on the top of my foot. My terror grew as I pulled off my shoe and sock and saw a row of red marks across the top of my foot. Inside my sock was a dead insect. Now I didn't know a wheel bug from a dung beetle, but there was a science teacher who had lived in Bolivia for about seven years. He would know. I carefully gathered the dead insect from my sock and put it in a glass jar and took it to him. He told me it was not a wheel bug. I was so relieved I didn't hear another word he said.

One other episode occurred which did threaten my life. It was the enigua incident. An enigua is a worm about two centimeters in length and as thick as a pencil lead. It enters the feet of people who walk barefoot. Usually I was very careful, but one night I got up and was too lazy to put on my slippers. About two weeks later, I felt a hard knot on the bottom of my foot. When I examined my foot, I saw a small, dark worm curled up inside a translucent cyst. The worm itself is not dangerous: it lays its eggs and dies. The problem is when the eggs hatch, the young eat their way up the leg. I knew it had to be cut out. I asked Al about it, since he had had one cut out of his foot a week earlier. He told me the doctor had charged him fifty dollars to perform the surgery. I didn't want to pay fifty dollars for something as simple as this, so I had a brilliant idea: I'd do it myself.

Now surgery should never be entered into lightly, especially if you are the one performing the surgery. Everything had to be planned carefully. Since I taught biology, I had access to a scalpel and alcohol. All I needed was an anesthetic. I didn't have any local anesthetic, so a general anesthetic would have to do. The only one I could think of was Bolivian beer. I was already acquainted with the anesthetic qualities of the local brew, so I had a pretty good idea of the dosage required. After I drank one liter of beer, I began the surgery. I needed to be able to complete the operation before I finished the second liter, after which there was a very real possibility of me chopping off a toe due to a loss of coordination. The operation was a complete success. Sometimes I wonder how I survived my time in Bolivia.

One of the more creepy phenomena happened around Christmas time. This was the hottest and most humid time of year, and since I didn't have air conditioning, mold started growing everywhere: on my cotton pillow cases, my leather belt, even my wooden chess set! It would not grow on my polyester pants, however. One last episode should be recounted here. One night I got up and saw this colossal cockroach on the floor. This thing was the size of a dump truck! I stepped on it and heard a sickening crunch. Since I was still very sleepy, I figured I would wait until morning to clean up the remains. The next morning, when I looked at the spot where where it had been crunched, it was gone! Following a faint trail of fluid, I saw to my horror that it had climbed the wall next to my bed. In another few minutes, this cockroach from Hell would have leapt off the wall and eaten my face.

THE SQUARE

On Saturday mornings, I would head for the *Plaza 24 de Septiembre*. It was a small park (one city block) in the middle of the first ring. The first thing I would do when I arrived, was search the trees for the sloths which lived there. It always gave me great pleasure to see them hanging lazily from the branches. On Saturdays and Sundays, families could be seen walking through the park during the day, and at night, young people in their late teens would stroll around the park, girls walking clockwise and boys counterclockwise, checking each other out. The locals called them *piraña*.

After watching the sloths for a while, I would stop by a newsstand just off the square and buy a copy of Time® magazine to catch up on the news from the States. Then I would go to the El Presidio Café, order a cup of coffee and roll, and watch the people as they passed by. The Presidio was across the street from the park, so it was a great place to watch people, especially from one of the tables on the sidewalk. Some of the most interesting and unexpected were the Mennonites. There were three Mennonite communities in the area surrounding Santa Cruz and they would come into town on Saturdays to sell the cheese they made and buy supplies. The men were distinctive with their beards, straw hats, and overalls. The women always wore aprons and head scarves.

Inevitably, some of the teachers from school would pass by. If they didn't have any pressing business, they might sit down, and we could spend hours talking and drinking coffee. Shoeshine boys worked the café, and for a nickel you could have your shoes shined. After the first shoe was shined, they would tap your shoe with the brush, to indicate it was time to put the other shoe on the box. These young boys were very creative businessmen: one time, a shoeshine boy wanted to shine my tennis shoes!

There was also a barbershop on the square, where I had my hair cut. They had an atomizer filled with alcohol which they would ignite with a lighter. The barber would place the comb and scissors into the flame of this mini blowtorch and make a show of killing all the insects and diseases which might live on the comb. A tobacco shop was two doors down from the barbershop. It was the only place in Santa Cruz where I could always find pipe tobacco. If I needed to pay my phone bill, the telephone company was also on the square. Occasionally, I would stop by the hardware store to buy lab supplies for school such as switches or hook up wire.

On the corner opposite El Presidio was a beautiful red brick cathedral built in the early 1600's. The post office was also on the square. My only regret is that I never went in to buy some of the beautiful stamps. The Casa de la Cultura was on the opposite side of the square where many local groups came to sing, dance, and make other presentations of local culture. Next door to that was an ice cream shop where ice cream could be purchased topped with rum (not rum flavoring). Finally, one of the favorite hang outs for the teachers was a place called Central Chop which was just off the square. It was a small bar that sold draft beer and was a great place to watch people.

CHICHA AND SAPO

L anguage differences can pose challenges and make life interesting for someone whose conversation is limited to simple phrases. One time I had some information I wanted to keep on the blackboard for a few days. I wrote "Do not erase" on the board. When I returned the next day, the board had been cleaned. I mentioned this to Larry, and he told me Felix, our custodian, didn't understand English. The next day, I wrote "*No bore*" on the board. The following day, it was perfectly clean again! When I asked Larry about this, he said, "Oh, Felix can't read." After that, when I wanted anything done, I would tell Felix in person, and everything was fine.

Felix was an excellent custodian, willing to do anything that was asked of him and always cheerful. He was always smiling, not the vacuous smile of someone who had undergone a lobotomy, but the smile of a person who has true inner peace and happiness. One Saturday

Felix invited Larry, Dan, Al, and me to visit his home in Jorochito, about thirty five kilometers southwest of Santa Cruz on the Cochabamba highway. We all piled into the school van and made the forty five minute trip to Jorochito.

When we arrived, we turned down a side road, and passed through a large wooden gate. The area inside the gate was completely enclosed. The back half of this area was surrounded by brick and mud houses all abutting one another with a *tienda* in the center of the back side. From the houses at the two ends, a red brick wall about three meters high enclosed the rest of the area. The area inside the gate was open and consisted mainly of tan colored dirt with a scattering of banana, papaya, and tangerine trees. It was about the size of two football fields. Chickens, pigs, and children ran around freely within this area. I figured the purpose of the wall was to keep their animals confined, as opposed to keeping the jungle animals out. Perhaps thirty to forty families lived there.

Tables had been brought out and were set up in the shade. We were introduced to some of Felix's friends and neighbors. We sat down at the tables all of which had pitchers of *chicha*, which is a fermented corn drink with about the same alcoholic content as wine. We sat around talking and drinking *chicha* in the shade as the tropical sun beat down all around us. About half an hour later, food was brought out and put on the tables. We had pork, chicken, and fried yucca. It was delicious!

We spent the rest of the afternoon playing *sapo. Sapo,* which means toad, is a game of skill played by two teams. The target was a wooden toad with saucer-sized holes cut out for the mouth, eyes, and other body parts. These holes had different values. We stood back five to ten meters from the target and tossed lead pellets about the size of four nickels glued together, trying to hit the holes. The four of us Americans were on one team, and the villagers on the other. We lost every game we played, but I do remember making the high score on one round. The day passed too quickly, and soon it was time for us to leave, but I'll always remember the day I spent in Jorochito as one of most relaxing in my life.

BACKPACKING THROUGH
SOUTH AMERICA

⌒∽⌒

The structure of this chapter is different from others in this book. It is essentially a direct transcription of a journal I kept on our three week trip across South America. This was written almost thirty years ago.

18 Dec 81

We left Santa Cruz two hours and fifty five minutes late. Getting onto the airplane was a joke: at one time there was a line, but it disintegrated into a mob of half-crazed people pushing and shoving to get on the plane. It seems most Bolivians have no concept of waiting in line. The flight to La Paz was uneventful, except for a little turbulence just before we reached La Paz. As soon as we started walking off the plane, we could tell we were at a much higher altitude than Santa Cruz. It was nothing more than a slight sense of weakness. The air was refreshingly chilly.

When we got into the airport terminal, a gentleman with a clipboard (he seemed to be acting in some sort of an official capacity) asked us if we had a place to stay and told us where we could change money. We got some city maps at the information counter and went out to catch a taxi. The taxi driver whipped a screwdriver out of his pocket and used it to open his trunk. The highway from the airport to La Paz is a toll road with a four lane divided highway with controlled access (the only one I've seen in Bolivia!). The highway is about 5 miles long and drops about one thousand feet. Coming down the highway we could see the lights of La Paz. It was spectacular, as if someone had sprinkled the lights all over the valley and the mountain sides. The place where we were staying, the Residencial Rosario, is located in the historic center of La Paz. From the outside it looked grungy, and when we were told that there were only communal bathrooms, I thought of all the sleazy bus terminal bathrooms I had seen in the States. I was pleasantly surprised; there is approximately one bathroom for every three rooms, and they are all very clean. The rooms are unheated, but the beds are piled high with llama hair blankets. The stairways are of different lengths, in different orientations, and go to all sorts of different levels. It reminds me of one of Escher's drawings. There is a small, but very nice, restaurant downstairs, and we had a late evening snack of hot vegetable soup and *té de coca* (a tea made from the leaves of the cocaine plant that is reportedly a good remedy for altitude sickness, we'll see).

19 Dec 81

It's an overcast day, with the clouds covering the upper reaches of the city. There seem to be a lot of foreigners staying here, mostly French and German. We had a very nice breakfast of fresh pineapple juice, hot rolls with butter and jelly, and coffee and *té de coca*. We were told that to prevent altitude sickness when walking in La Paz, to walk very slowly (like you are seventy years old). Symptoms of altitude sickness can range from dizziness to pulmonary edema. The *té de coca* seems to work, but the effects may be psychological. We did a lot of walking today, a little over four miles (all this at 12,000 feet!). We went to the train station and found out the soonest we could get out of town was next Friday. Then we went to the bus station, but the window of the office we wanted was closed. Next we took a taxi to the money changers, but they didn't have any Chilean pesos. After that we walked to Braniff's offices, but there were no flights to Chile for over a week. It's almost impossible to get out of La Paz this time of year. We walked back to our hotel, the 20 and 30 story skyscrapers were as impressive against the backdrop of the Andes as the steep side streets were tiring. From our hotel we walked back toward the center of town where we stopped at a bookstore and bought a copy of Time® magazine. Then it was on to the Lloyd Aero Boliviano offices where we found out that we'd have to come back at 3 pm to make reservations for the flight to Arica, Chile. We had a leisurely hour and a half lunch at El Meson which included an impressive palm heart salad and an avocado salad. Then we returned to the LAB offices where we found out that the next flight was booked solid, and we'd have to wait for over a week for the next flight. As we walked back to the hotel, we saw an Indian woman with a blanket spread on the ground selling candy, key chains, and Rubic's Cubes®! We decided to check the buses tomorrow. All of the walking had left us exhausted, so we took a siesta, got up, ate supper, and went to bed for a good night's sleep.

20 Dec 81

We got up at six. I took a shower with warm water that dribbled out of the shower, got dressed, and went out to take some pictures in the early morning. After I got back, we had a nice breakfast, and then I walked to the bus station only to find out that the bus had left at 8 am. Walking back, I discovered how easy it was to navigate around La Paz. Returning to the hotel, we decided to get a cup of coffee. Then we walked to the train station, but the tickets we wanted go on sale Monday. We walked down to the Prado to find an American newspaper, couldn't find one, so we ate lunch, checked out the theaters for movies, and returned to the hotel for a nap. After an hour I got up and went out to look for a *cuaderno*. I couldn't find one so I stopped in a restaurant. While I was there I met a family from Santa Cruz. While we were talking I found out that they knew John Dunston from the New Orleans bar! I walked back to the hotel, then we went out to see a movie, but we were early, so we stopped by the Don Quijote Bar for a drink. Then we went to see "Battle of the Titans". Afterwards we stopped by the hotel restaurant for soup and sandwiches.

21 Dec 81

We got up bright and early and after breakfast, went to the train station to see if we could get tickets to Antofagasta. Luck was with us and we were able to get first class tickets for only $20- each! Before returning to the hotel, I bought a *cuaderno* for some games I had invented. After about 15 minutes, we left to go to the American embassy to find out what we needed to do because the exit date on our passports had expired. As we walked in two Bolivian soldiers came to attention and gave us a snappy salute. It really made me feel important. The embassy gave us the address of the immigration office and told us that we'd have to go down there. We took a taxi down to immigration, and surprise of surprises, it only took an hour of time and no money to have our exit dates extended by six days! There were other people getting their passports processed as well. Two of the passports I saw had money inside. It seemed to me that that might be interpreted by some people as a bribe. It turned out that is exactly what was intended. A Chilean was told by the officials that his name was on a list (what list I don't know) and that his passport couldn't be processed. A few minutes later this guy hands the official his passport, the official put the passport in his lap, then I saw him put some money into his front pants pocket (I can't say for sure the money came from the passport; it may have been lying on the official's lap and he decided that that particular moment was a good time to put it in a safer place.), then he stamped the passport, and the guy was on his way. After immigration, we took a taxi uptown and ate lunch at Gargantua's. Since we had four more days in La Paz, we thought it might be nice to take a tour of the city, so we checked at a tour agency next door to Gargantua's. Then we went back to the hotel and played some of the games I invented and some Spill-'n'-Spell®, ate supper, and turned in early.

22 Dec 81

We got up bright and late, ate breakfast, and returned to the room to plan our strategy for the day. About 11:30 we went downtown to buy some pesos. We got 39 pesos to the dollar, over 50% higher than the official rate! (They love those greenbacks.) While I was there I saw this lady behind the counter count up $1,000 in United States currency. I've never seen so many bucks in my life. Then we went to the tour agency and paid $7.50 apiece for the afternoon's tour of La Paz. Then we stopped at Burger King for lunch. Well it wasn't exactly Burger King, everything looked right except for the logo. Instead of "Burger King" between the two buns, it said "Pumper Nic", and they called French fries "frenys". I had a couple of beers with my 'burger and fries (you can't do that at Burger King!). It was nice to have a taste of the States after so long. We spent about an hour walking on the Prado waiting for our tour to begin. The tour was very enjoyable. We visited the Indian market, the black market (which covered ten square blocks), the witches' market (with their llama fetuses), and San Francisco church (which was built in 1548). The inside of the church would knock your eyes out. The wealth and workmanship in praise of God is something you'd have to see to appreciate. One interesting point about the church is that the outside is decorated with Inca gods, including the goddess Mother Earth (*pacha mama*). Then we visited the Murillo museum which contained a lot of artifacts from both the early Spanish and Indian cultures. Then we got to see the Bolivian parliament building and the soccer stadium (both from the outside). Going to "Moon Valley" we got a view of Mt. Illimani, the spectacular 21,000+ foot peak near La Paz. "Moon Valley" is about ten miles from downtown La Paz. It is heavily eroded sandstone and shale that form weird spires, bridges, and sinkholes. The whole region covers about 50 acres. We got to see the Bolivian Military Academy (the "Presidents' School"), and drove through a few different residential areas. We also got to see a natural preservation area where about 99% of all known species of Bolivian cacti grow. The trip back into town followed a different route, so we had the opportunity to see quite a bit of La Paz. At the end of the tour they dropped us off at our hotel, so we didn't have to make the uphill trip on foot. After a pleasant supper, we ended a very busy day.

23 Dec 81

After breakfast, we waited about fifteen minutes freezing our buns off for the tour bus to pick us up. We took the *autopista* up to the airport and then set off across the Altiplano to Tiwanaku. The Altiplano is impressive in its desolation. The natural landscape of little more than broom grass is broken up by small plots of land farmed by the Indians, growing potatoes, onions, and some grains. The Altiplano reminds me of traveling across Wyoming from Rawlins to Green River or of the scenes from the movie "Dr. Zhivago" portraying the Russian steppes. When we finally reached Tiwanaku, I didn't realize we were there. You don't know what to look for, only the chain link fence surrounding the site gives it away. I'm not going to describe the ruins we saw (you have to see them to get a feel of the impact of the ruins). Perhaps the best way to describe them is to give a historical account of Tiwanaku. Of the two major Indian languages of Bolivia, the Tiwanaku group spoke Aymara and the Incas spoke Quechua. The civilization at Tiwanaku pre-dated the Roman civilization by one thousand years, and the Inca civilization by 1,500 years! This was no fly-by-night civilization: they had plumbing and had mastered the use of gold, silver, lead, copper, and bronze and had an empire that stretched from Ecuador to Argentina. After

2,500 years of existence, the civilization suddenly came to an end for reasons which archaeologists are uncertain of (around 1,000 AD). About three hundred years after the end of the Tiwanaku civilization, the Incas first came into this area. The Tiwanaku people were still living among the ruins of the temples, but could tell the Incas nothing of the history! It's a mystery Von Däniken would have a field day with. The trip back was as enjoyable as the trip out. When we got on the *autopista* to descend to La Paz, the driver stopped so we could take pictures of La Paz in the bowl shaped valley below. After the tour, we had lunch at a Chinese restaurant where we had some of the best egg rolls I've ever eaten. After lunch, we returned to the hotel, took a long siesta, ate supper, and went to bed.

24 Dec 81

Tomorrow we leave for Chile, so today we didn't do much. At breakfast there was a nice surprise when the owner of the hotel and restaurant gave us a Christmas card. We passed the time in the morning playing games, and then we had a nice lunch of salad, soup, meat, potatoes, rice, and tea for less than $1.50 per person! In the afternoon we went to the Indian market to buy items for our train trip: we got bananas, avocados, raisins, candy, toilet paper, and a llama hair blanket. The blanket only cost seven dollars. We rested up the rest of the afternoon. During supper the restaurant was packed, so we shared our table with an Australian who was touring South America. Wandering around the hotel after supper, I found a nice view of the city from the third floor. Just before bed, as I was coming back from the bathroom, I could hear the people in the church next door singing "Silent Night". Under the stars that chilly night it sounded really nice.

25 Dec 81 Christmas Day

By 8:15 in the morning, we were packed and ready to go. We went down for breakfast and had fresh watermelon juice along with our usual fare. It's nice and sunny today. We just figured that in the week we've been in La Paz, we've walked a minimum of 24 miles, half of that uphill, all at an altitude of 12,000 feet! We got to the train station about an hour early, our train was there, so we were able to board, unfortunately our coach number wasn't on the train. I talked to the station manager and he found out that the wrong coach number was on our ticket, so he fixed everything up. It took about 40 minutes to go from lower La Paz to the Altiplano. On the way we passed through a eucalyptus forest and had several excellent views of La Paz. When we reached the Altiplano about an hour out of La Paz, they disconnected the dining car from the train! There is no way to get anything to eat or drink until we reach Chile. Fortunately, the train stops at many of the small villages along the way, and Indian women get on board selling stew from steaming pots. It is made with beef, carrots, onions, curly-cue pasta, and *chuños*. *Chuños* are freeze dried potatoes. They are not dried commercially, but placed outside in the cold dry air of the Altiplano, in a process thousands of years old. It is served in a cone made from old newspapers, and it's delicious! It was a great meal for ten pesos (50 cents). The Altiplano is flat and more or less barren with villages strung out along the railroad tracks with no apparent reason for their existence. We had a magnificent view of Illimani going away from La Paz. Most of the railroad bed is built up about three feet above the ground level as much of this part of the Altiplano is subject to periodic flooding even though the rainfall here is only 8 inches a year. There are quite a few llamas casually munching beside the railroad tracks. The train ride across the Altiplano must be like it was traveling across the American frontier one hundred years ago. In the seat across from us is an Indian woman with a baby tightly wrapped in layer after layer of blankets. The baby is so tightly wound, I don't know how it can breathe. There's a huge marsh (about one hundred square miles) just south of Oruro with swamp grass, ducks, and other birds. I think I'll try to catch some shuteye.

26 Dec 81

It's one o'clock in the morning, and we've been waiting in this little town for an hour (for another train, I think). It's very hard for me to sleep in wooden seats that don't recline. Here comes the train now. It's five thirty in the morning and is light outside. Up ahead is Uyuni, where the rail line divides, with one line going to Antofagasta,

Chile and one going to Buenos Aires, Argentina. There is still flat land with hundreds of square miles of salt flats (larger than the Great Salt Lake desert, in fact the largest in the world). The land is barren with occasional patches of moss. Now we're waiting at the Chilean border. When we got off the train, a llama came up and started licking our hands. We fed it some crackers. We've been here an hour and will be here about one more hour. I think we're waiting for a Chilean train so we can change coaches. We're sitting here passing the time with an American, a German, and a Japanese. After waiting two and a half hours, the engine finally came and took us across the border into Chile. There's a volcano on the Bolivian-Chilean border, and Linda noticed that it is still smoking. Well, we waited three hours on the Chilean side of the border for customs. We all had to get out of the train and line up. When it was our turn to be searched, he asked us if we were tourists, and when we said yes, told us to go back to the train without even searching us. After we left the border, we went by several volcanoes and a huge dry salt lake bed which was covered with a thick layer of nitrates. We climbed up to 12,800 feet and began our descent to sea level, which we will reach in only 230 miles! They gave us bus tickets to Antofagasta from Calama because they are repairing the rail line between those two cities. We just passed Chuquicamata, which is the largest open pit copper mine in the world. At Calama we had to find the bus ourselves because nobody told us anything. I hope they're going to have hotels waiting for us when we reach Antofagasta, because it's almost midnight.

27 Dec 81

It's two thirty in the morning, and here we are in Antofagasta. The bus station is closed, the hotels are closed, and we don't have a place to stay. Fortunately, there are six of us in the same boat: a Japanese, two Germans, and three Americans. We found a place still open and the six of us had a cup of hot tea. When we were six or seven blocks from the ocean, I could smell it, and it smelled good! We found a place on the beach where the six of us could sleep. We're up against a sea wall, surrounding our packs, so everything should be O.K. A couple of guys cane down to the beach with an inner tube. They found a pallet and lashed it to the inner tube. I guess they think they're going to sail around the world. One guy came up and asked us something, but the ocean was too loud, so I asked him what he wanted. When I asked him what he wanted, it woke all the others up (everyone had gone to sleep, and I was the only one who heard this guy). Now I'm worried, everyone is sound asleep like they were safe in a hotel. Oh well, it's only two and a half hours to daylight. Another pair of guys came down to the beach with an inner tube. They're going fishing for something. One of them was pounding rocks together for about five minutes (I don't know why), anyway after a couple of minutes, one of the guys wakes up and says, "What's that." I was so pissed off because I was the only one awake guarding our stuff and our lives I felt like saying, "It's nothing, just a killer knifing the German," but I didn't. There's a boat in the bay, close to the land with a bright light. At first I imagined it was a smuggler because about 100 yards from us was a guy standing in the shadows smoking a cigarette, I couldn't see him, but I saw the glowing end of his cigarette. Later I realized that he was part of the fishing operation. It's six thirty and light, and there are sandpipers and seagulls flying around, and the ocean sounds nice. I'm going to sleep. It's seven thirty, and everyone else is still racked out. I might as well get up and walk around. Antofagasta is beautiful. There are all sorts of different shells on the beach. Everyone finally got up, and around nine we all went across the street for breakfast. There is a weird hotel here: all of the rooms are converted buses. A few of the others want to check out a cheaper place to stay, but I'm whipped. I'm getting some sleep here. Around two in the afternoon I got up, and we went out and found a restaurant that served seafood. While we were there we met an English girl who was traveling around South America. We gorged ourselves on seafood, and then checked out downtown Antofagasta. It's beautiful and modern. We spent the afternoon on the on the beach. There was an ice cream vendor on the beach, and as he walked, he would yell out, *"¡Rico! ¡Riquismo!"* We watched the tide come in and the sun set. Then we had a drink and went to bed.

28 Dec 81

After breakfast, we got a map of Antofagasta, changed some money, and got bus tickets to Santiago. We went back to the restaurant where we stopped for tea that first night. The owner was really pleased that we came back, evidently, none of the others did. We had a delicious clam lunch with a nice salad made with lemon juice instead of vinegar. We spent an enjoyable hour watching the ocean and then walked up to the bus station to catch our bus to Santiago. Climbing out of Antofagasta, I was surprised how quickly desert totally dominated the landscape. The bus driver took our passports. (It turned out he was to keep them for the entire 800 mile trip to Santiago to show at the various military checkpoints. I still don't like the idea of someone else keeping my passport when I'm in a foreign country!) The Atacama desert is one of the driest places on earth. For hundreds of miles there is nothing but dirt and rock, not a blade of grass, not a piece of moss. Along the road in northern Chile are about 70 roadside shrines. Every time we pass one, the bus driver waves at it, like he was saying "hi" to some trucker's soul. Around 8:30 we stopped for supper. We ate cow stomach, rice, and bread, and drank tea. (The meal was included in the price of the bus ticket.) Just before midnight (at the edge of the Atacama desert), we stopped at a fruit and vegetable inspection station. We all had to get off the bus, and all of our baggage was searched.

29 Dec 81

The region south of the Atacama desert is still desert, but it's more like west Texas, with cactus, yucca, and sagebrush growing. There are also a lot of hawks around here. There are trees and grain crops in the valleys where they use irrigation. About 9 o'clock, we stopped for breakfast. As we go farther and farther south, we see more and more fruit trees. Going into Santiago, Chile from the north is not very exciting. We descended from the mountains into a broad, flat plane. There is quite a bit of smog in the air. The bus station in Santiago is a zoo. There are about fifteen guys yelling, "Taxi!" at everyone who gets off the bus, and you have to tell them, "no" to their face, because you are too stupid to figure out that they're offering taxis to you unless you answer yes or no. We got a pop sickle from a street vendor and then walked about ten blocks and found a suitable hotel called the Ritz. It's located about half a block from Huerfanos. Huerfanos is a street, that for about 15 blocks, has been converted into a pedestrian mall. It's beautiful, with flowers and trees planted all around and lined with all sorts of nifty shops (including a Pierre Cardin store), movie theaters, and eating places. We stopped for a delicious pizza and a typical Chilean salad of tomatoes, onion, olive oil, and lemon juice. While walking, we passed a Kentucky Fried Chicken® place. We saw "Raiders of the Lost Ark" at one of the theaters on the mall and then retired for the evening.

30 Dec 81

We got up about nine and went to the seventh floor restaurant. Then we went to the bus station to get tickets to Curicó. Going there we rode on the subway. The Santiago subway system is beautiful, clean, and efficient. There are trains running in both directions every three minutes, and every car has at least two maps of the system so you can tell where you are going. In addition to that, each station has the station name in big letters posted ten times on each side of the tracks. It was so nice, that after we got our bus tickets, we rode the subway to one end and then crossed over the tracks, and took it back to the junction and then rode the spur to the end. (You can do that because once you get into the train area, you can use an overpass at any station to cross over and take the subway back. Theoretically, you could ride all day on all branches for only 25 cents.) Then we went to send a telegram to Joanne to tell her we'd be arriving in Llico the next day. (Joanne is my principal's wife, and she invited us to stay at her parent's house when we visited Chile.) Next, we walked up to the top of Santa Lucia hill and then went to San Cristobal. San Cristobal is the highest hill in Santiago with a castle on top. We took a steep inclined railway to the top and then grabbed a snack at a snack bar. Then we took an aerial tramway to the midpoint of the mountain. We stopped by a bar for a leisurely drink, while enjoying a spectacular view of the city. Then we walked around visiting the swimming pool, the mountain top restaurant, and a wine tasting cellar. San Cristobal also has many paths for walking, children's playgrounds, a police dog training academy, a zoo, and botanical gardens. We returned to our hotel and went to Fritz's for supper. On the way back to our hotel, we stopped for a while to watch a mime perform on the mall. Then we returned to the hotel and enjoyed a well deserved sleep.

31 Dec 81

We woke up at 6:00 am, packed, and took the subway to the bus station. We had time for coffee and rolls, and then we boarded the bus for Curicó. South of Santiago, the countryside is filled with orchards and vineyards; it's breathtaking. Once we arrived in Curicó, we had a six block walk to the place where the Llico bus leaves. This town is full of old-time horse drawn buggies. We got our tickets, but had a four-hour wait, so we went to a restaurant. I noticed a Peter Frampton poster on the wall of the restaurant. We sat outside in a grape arbor with bunches of grapes hanging down everywhere. While we were eating our seafood lunch, a goat was lead through the restaurant to the kitchen. I think he was destined to become supper. After waiting a while at the bus station, we boarded the bus and were on our way to Llico. The four-hour trip to Llico is curvy, bumpy, and dusty. It is slow too. The four-hour trip covers less than 120 kilometers. (I counted 13 stops in one half-hour period!) The countryside changed from vineyards and orchards to pine forests as we crossed the coast range. Llico has a beautiful lake with swans swimming in a small area of the lake. The lake is separated from the Pacific Ocean by a sand bar about five meters high and twenty meters wide. Later I found out the lake had been sounded by Charles Darwin on his expedition with the *Beagle*. Eventually, everyone got off the bus, until we were the only two left. We finally had to get off because we were at the end of the line. We didn't see Joanne, but a gentleman who knew Joanne's father drove us to their house. Joanne was really surprised to see us (she had not received our telegram). We had a delicious dinner of mussels with wine, talked a while, and settled down for a good night's sleep.

1 Jan 82 New Year's day

I got up early and walked down to the lake. It sure was peaceful with the fog slowly rising off the lake and the pine trees all around. Then I walked down the road a way and took a few photographs. When I returned to the house, everyone else was getting up, and we had a nice breakfast. After breakfast, Joanne took us out in the boat for a tour of the lake. It was a beautiful hour and a half trip that took us by a minimum of 150 $100,000 homes. The lake was dotted with scores of sail boats and many motor boats. I can see why Joanne loves it so much here. After lunch, we walked about three miles to the ocean. It was cold and windy, but even under those conditions the ocean is enchanting. Perhaps it is mankind's heritage of the ocean that draws us so strongly to it. After supper, we retired in preparation for tomorrow's early rising.

2 Jan 82

It's just getting light outside. We hate to leave Llico, but there are worlds out there waiting for us to explore. Joanne and her father took us down to the bus and saw us off. The trip back to Curicó was uneventful, but it was spectacular in it's beauty. We walked across the plaza to the train station after reaching Curicó and got tickets to Chillan. At Chillan we will be able to make connections south. The railway line from Curicó to Chillan is electric and very smooth and comfortable. The landscape is a feast for the eyes. During our trip south we passed an air liquefaction plant, and it had tanks for nitrogen, oxygen, and argon. At Chillan we have an eight and a half hour wait for connections south, so we went to the park, and then to a restaurant for lunch. Chillan is the birthplace of Bernardo O'Higgins who was Chile's liberator. We got a hotel after lunch, so we'd get some rest, and then we walked to the train station to catch our train south. The train is a pleasure, reclining seats with blankets, everything clean and modern. Just as we were getting to sleep, the conductor told us that there was a mistake, and we should really be in the first class section and not in the second class section. We picked up our packs and gladly followed him through the dining car, through two grungy looking cars, and then to the end of the train.

This can't be right, we were better off in second class. So we talked to the conductor and found out that they had sold us the wrong tickets by accident and we actually had second class tickets. We paid 500 extra pesos and got our old seats back.

3 Jan 82

Sometime during the night the train switched from electric to diesel, but I don't know when. It's light now, and the countryside is mostly trees dotted with fields. The rolling tree covered hills remind me of the Ozarks of northwest Arkansas. Going into Osorno, there is a beautiful cathedral painted yellow and red that overlooks the town. Osorno sits on the banks of a beautiful lake. The train followed the shore of the lake into Puerto Montt, where the tracks end (this is the southernmost railway station in the world). We got off the train and were met by an urchin who gave us all these cards of hotels in the area and then led us to a hotel. He told us it was 800 pesos a night, and as we got to the hotel, he ducked in the door and said, "*ocho cientos*", so I figured that the price was cheaper. My theory was reinforced when the urchin told us we didn't have to tip him (he probably gets a cut of the overage). I didn't mind; he performed a useful service for us, and we have a pleasant, clean room with a nice view. After we settled in, we decided to catch a bus and get some grub. The bus went all over Puerto Montt and ended up dropping us off only ten blocks from where we started, but we got a nice tour of the city. The architecture of Puerto Montt is amazing: steep roofs and balconies reminiscent of Switzerland. The first restaurant we went to was closed (the owner was going to the beach), the second didn't have a menu, and when we asked what kind of food they had, told us they didn't have any food! The third was closed. The fourth only had soup and potatoes with meat (no specification of the type of meat, just meat). We went into a funky restaurant that served seafood that looked, felt, and tasted like beef. (In fact, if I ate fish in that restaurant, I'd like biologists to investigate it, because I ate a fish unknown to mankind!) Stuffed with food, we wandered back to the hotel and took a siesta. After the nap, we went around the corner for a sea food dinner and then we sacked out.

4 Jan 82

We got up, had breakfast, cleaned up, and then went out to get tickets to San Carlos de Bariloche. We changed $120- and then stopped at a restaurant for cake and coffee. We walked along the beach and watched the seagulls, and then had lunch at a German restaurant. It had a spectacular view of the ocean. The television at the bar was on, and they were watching an old episode of "Kung Fu" in Spanish. Linda had a Chilean salad, and I had a delicious lunch of oysters on the half shell and beer. Linda went back to the hotel for a nap, and I went to the German restaurant for a beer. With the German music in the background and the surroundings, including a huge World War II map of Germany on the wall, I feel like I'm in Germany. Then I walked down the beach for almost a mile. I went out along a jetty. At the jetty there was a plaque telling how much of the city had been destroyed by an earthquake and how the United States helped to rebuild it. I went back to the hotel. After a while, we went out for a delicious seafood dinner.

5 Jan 82

We got up early to catch the 8 o'clock bus out of Puerto Montt. The bus trip was pleasant. The landscape starts out with rolling grasslands which change to tree-covered hills and finally to the pine-covered Andes. Crossing the Andes this far south is easier than a more northern passage, as the Andes are only 8,000-10,000 feet in altitude here. This area is the famous "lake country" of Chile and Argentina. With the pine trees, lakes, and log cabins, it's just like being in Idaho or Utah. Crossing the border from Chile to Argentina was uneventful, although we did have about an hour's wait at the border. About 1:30 in the afternoon, we stopped for lunch at a café. We didn't have any Argentine pesos, so I asked if $US would be alright. No problem. We had a sandwich and a Coke®. I gave the waitress a twenty dollar bill, and she kept giving me 10,000 peso notes for change. It was then that I found out that the exchange rate was 10,000 to 1!! After lunch our bus trip continued. We traveled about three fourths of the way around this large lake and passed extinct volcanoes. The scenery was spectacular. About twelve miles outside of San Carlos de Bariloche, our bus stopped at a military checkpoint. All foreigners had to check with the police and let them know what hotel they were staying in. I told them since we hadn't arrived in town yet, I didn't know. He wrote down something in a big book, and let us continue on our way. Bariloche is the most beautiful little city I have ever seen. It is on the shore of a large lake and in the foothills of the Andes. It is a ski resort, and about 1/3 to 1/2 of the people we see are college age, many of them wearing ski clothes. The architecture has a strong Swiss influence. There are flower boxes and small parks all over the city. After getting settled in our hotel, getting a map of the city, and changing $120- (that's over one million pesos!), we went out to eat supper. We had Argentine steak and baked potatoes with bleu cheese instead of butter. It was delicious.

6 Jan 82

One of the first orders of business after breakfast (a meager fare of hard rolls, butter, jelly, and coffee), was to make arrangements to get to Buenos Aires, since we have tickets to fly out of Buenos Aires in three days. After checking around, our best bet seems to be the Patagonian Express, a 40 hour trip across Patagonia and the Pampas by rail. We wandered around Bariloche and saw all sorts of interesting things. On the plaza near the lake is a Swiss clock tower.

Near that is a castle-like wall that is about 16 feet thick that has two arches in it so that cars can drive through. We stopped by a tea room for tea and pastries. After that we went into a chocolate shop that literally had hundreds of kinds of chocolate: black, white, brown, ribbons, bars, blocks, with nuts, liquor, etc. Linda bought over a quarter of a million pesos worth of chocolate. We walked around some more and visited a nice park with lots of flowers. Then we went back to our hotel for a siesta. Later that evening, we had a nice dinner.

7 Jan 82

After breakfast, we started getting ready for the next leg of our trip. We bought some fruit and filled our canteen with water. Then we caught a taxi to the train station. The train really looked nice, and the seats were comfortable with lots of room. We pulled out of the station about four o'clock and made a slow climb out of the valley. Looking back at the Andes was one of the most impressive sights I've ever seen. The snow-covered peaks were steep and jagged, almost like church spires. Our first stop in Patagonia was a village that couldn't have had a population of more than two hundred. There were a few gauchos in typical dress waiting for the train. Patagonia is similar to the semi-arid region of Wyoming with scrub grass and sagebrush used for sheep grazing. There are occasional outcrops of rock in the form of hills and mesas, but basically it is flat. We walked to the dining car, which is the only air-conditioned car on the train. Except for a table with a few Argentine soldiers, we were the only ones in the dining car. Our waiter looked exactly like Steve Martin!! We half expected him to come to our table with a fake arrow in his head. We had a beer and a Coke®, then Linda went back to our car. I stayed, just thinking and watching the scenery. I don't think I have ever felt that tranquil in my entire life. I went back to my seat. A couple of hours later, we stopped at a fairly large town. I don't know the name of it. We waited for about an hour, probably so the train from Buenos Aires could pass us, since there is only a single track through Patagonia. While we were there, an old steam locomotive pulled up on the track next to us. I estimate that this town has a population of about 10,000. They are in the middle of Patagonia, and I doubt if they have any roads in or out of here, which means the only contact with the outside world is some ten trains a week. After we left that town, I started noticing a lot of dust in the air. Supper was fabulous. We had some type of rolled roast (It looked so good, I took a picture of it!) with some mashed potatoes and all sorts of relishes in it (it tasted like mashed potato salad) and wine. I stuffed myself with all these goodies, only to find out that they were only the appetizers!! The main meal was elegantly spiced chicken with mixed vegetables and bread. We were heartbroken because we were so full and could hardly eat any of it. Now that is what I call dining excellence! After supper we went back to our car to go to sleep. It was so dusty, we had to sleep with handkerchiefs over our mouths. We looked like a car full of bandits.

8 Jan 82

It's morning, and it's "dust city". When we hit our clothes, clouds of dust come off. There is dust all over the floor, on the seats, my hair is brown with dust, even the glasses I put in my pocket are covered with dust! I have never seen so much dust in my life. We are now in the region that is the boundary between Patagonia and the Pampas. The landscape is greener with an occasional tree. After breakfast we arrived in Bahía Blanca; it's on the Atlantic coast. We crossed over a large river on a very interesting bridge. It is a highway bridge with lines like a road, except that the railroad tracks run right down the middle of the road. When a train needs to cross, traffic is stopped at both ends of the bridge with crossing gates, and the train crosses. Then the bridge is used for cars and trucks again. The Pampas is just like I always imagined it to be. There are large wheat fields and groups of trees surrounding farm houses; just like Kansas. There are also some pastures with beef and dairy cattle grazing. The only clue that this is not Kansas, is the occasional rhea grazing along with the cattle beside the tracks. As we approach Buenos Aires, we notice more and more trees. There was a spectacular sunset on the Pampas that I got a picture of. Buenos Aires is huge, it took an hour and a half to get from the outskirts to the train station in downtown Buenos Aires. It was about midnight when we arrived at the train station. We caught a taxi to get to where we wanted to go, but the driver didn't know how to get there (he even asked some other cab drivers at traffic lights how to get there, but no one seemed to know). Finally he suggested a place, and since we were tired, we said okay. He dropped us off about two blocks from the hotel. We had to walk because the street had been converted into a pedestrian mall. (That seems to be popular in the large South American cities.) Even though it was after midnight, there were literally thousands of people walking on the mall, and the restaurants and cafés and bars were open. On the way to the hotel, we saw a crowd gathered to watch a lady sing. She was on a third floor balcony wearing an evening gown and had a small orchestra accompanying her. The front was all glassed in, and we heard the music through a loud speaker. It was quite unusual. We finally checked into our hotel.

9 Jan 82

Today is the last day of our trip. After breakfast, we walked down to the LAB office to verify our flight back to Santa Cruz. The size of Buenos Aires overwhelms me. I don't think I've ever seen so many taxicabs in my life! The main boulevard has six lanes both ways, and in the middle is a sidewalk with trees, flowers, and benches. There is a tall obelisk that is a landmark. It has four roads converging on it. We walked to a small park and took some pictures. Buenos Aires is a beautiful city, I wish we had about a week to spend here. We packed up our gear and caught a cab to the airport. The airport is way out of town. It took us forty minutes to get there but only cost us eight dollars. The taxi driver was really nice and told us all sorts of interesting things about the city. While waiting for the airplane, we had an hors d'oeuvre tray. I had a drink they called a martini; the only similarity to a real martini was the olive. Our plane trip back to Santa Cruz was uneventful. When we got off the plane, we noticed the humidity right away. Fortunately, it was unseasonably cool.

THE GREAT REFRIGERATOR CAPER

One of the consequences of living overseas is that you tend to spend a lot of time with other Americans. There are a couple of reasons for this. First was the cultural factor: it was nice to spend time with people who had similar interests and spoke English. The other was that we had a lot of time on our hands. Most of us left our friends and families back in the States, and we had no organizations or television to take up time.

Al, Jim, David, and I had spent most of Saturday down at Central Chop drinking beer, and since it was approaching curfew, Dave and Jim invited us to spend the night at their place. To prevent American teachers from being picked up by the police for curfew violation, any time it was close to midnight, the host or hostess would allow their guests to spend the night at their house. I don't know how many different homes I spent the night in while I was in Bolivia, or how many people spent the night at my place. This illustrates just how close-knit the American community was. (Actually, the punishment for curfew violation was not that severe. The police would take the lawbreaker down to the soccer stadium, put the miscreant's shoes in the middle of the playing field, and they would spend the entire night painting bleachers. At six o'clock, they found their shoes and went home.)

Jim and David had been friends for years. They met while they were teaching in Spain. We called them the Andersons (Jim's last name was Anderson and Dave's was Andersen). They had a very nice place near the square, but it was weird. A wrought iron gate separated the first floor hallway from the street. The hallway went back to an apartment on the first floor where another family lived. There was nothing else in the hallway except a refrigerator and a stairway going up one and a half stories to Jim and Dave's apartment. The top of the stairway opened to a covered walkway that looked down into a garden on the first floor. The walkway was covered in red tiles, and there was a railing along this walkway, to prevent people from falling into the garden. There were five doorways off this area that led to the kitchen, bathroom, living room, and two bedrooms (I said this was a weird apartment). We usually sat outside, along the walkway so we could enjoy the colorful birds that came to the papaya and mango trees in the garden.

The only problem with this paradise was that every time we wanted a beer, we had to down to the first floor for a new bottle. As the level of beer approached the bottom of the bottles, we had a slow beer drinking contest, because the first person finished would have to bring up a new bottle for everyone else. The loser was usually someone who could no longer stand to have a couple of centimeters of warm, flat beer in his bottle. This particular night, I could stand it no longer and asked Dave why he had never brought the refrigerator upstairs. He said it was too heavy for the two of them to bring it up by themselves, and they had never thought of moving it when they had company. We all looked at each other, and I said I thought we should bring it up now. There are many things that seem reasonable after a day of beer drinking that would not even be considered by a sober mind. This was one of those things.

We all reeled down the stairs and emptied the beer bottles from the refrigerator (those were the only items in there). This was a massive refrigerator, and we were not in the best condition to be moving a one hundred kilogram behemoth up a flight of stairs, but it seemed like a good idea at the time. After we unplugged it, we laid it over on its side, and each of us lifted up a corner. We staggered up the stairs under the tremendous load. It must have been quite comical to watch four drunken guys wrestle this huge refrigerator up a flight and a half of stairs. It's amazing that we only dropped it one time. When we arrived at the top, we collapsed on the floor gasping for air. After we spent five minutes recovering our breath, we moved the refrigerator into the kitchen and plugged it into the outlet. It worked!

We placed the bottles of beer back into the refrigerator, keeping four out for ourselves, and sat on the floor admiring our work. Jim told us he was going out tomorrow and buy something from one of the other food groups (besides beer) to put inside it. A week later, Dave told me the refrigerator was still running. Evidently, dropping it had no affect on how well it ran. The moral? I'm sure there must be one somewhere.

SAMAIPATA

~*~

None of us had cars in Bolivia, so we didn't have the opportunity to jump into our automobiles and go sightseeing at a moment's notice. Since we had to use public transportation, trips to the surrounding areas required some planning. One weekend, six of us decided to visit Samaipata, a small village in the Andean foothills. We rented a house for the weekend, and at 7:30 Saturday morning, Linda, her two roommates, Lisa and Betsy, and Jim, Dave, and I met at the bus station in downtown Santa Cruz.

The bus we boarded was small (it only held 20 passengers). Samaipata was 120 kilometers southwest of Santa Cruz on the Cochabamba Highway, so we were looking at a two or three hour trip. At the 15 kilometer checkpoint, we had to wait until the military cleared the bus for passage. While we were waiting, vendors came up to the windows outside the bus selling pineapples, roasted peanuts, *ganeos*, and other snacks. *Ganeos* are bananas about half the size of the bananas we are used to seeing back in the States. They never seemed to overripen so they were always firm and not sickeningly sweet, even if the outside was brown. All of us bought snacks for the trip.

As the road wound through the Amazon jungle, I was struck by the number of papaya trees that grew wild everywhere. Along the way, there were areas cleared out of the jungle for family dwellings. Some had thatched roofs, but most of the roofs were made of corrugated tin. There were a few of the ubiquitous papaya trees around the dwellings and a small clearing for a garden. Some had small fenced areas for chickens.

As we entered Samaipata, I saw a Pink Floyd poster pasted on one of the walls. On another wall, someone had painted Kiss with the characteristic lightning bolt s's. We exited the bus onto a dirt street. There were one story white buildings along both sides of the street, and pigs and chickens roamed freely. It was like a Hollywood portrayal of the quintessential Mexican village. The place where we were staying was about a ten minute walk from the bus station. It looked like a Swiss chalet or ski lodge and had sleeping accommodations for eight. There was a stack of wood piled up next to the fireplace.

Since Samaipata was a bit higher in elevation than Denver, the air was pleasantly cool and dry. After we had dropped our baggage at the house, we walked to town to a small shop and bought two liters of wine, some potatoes, a piece of beef, and vegetables for a dinner salad. We also purchased eggs, bread, and jam for breakfast.

After we dropped the food off at the house, we went into town to have lunch at a café. We spent about an hour sitting and chatting. After lunch, we decided to visit a local museum. It was quite small, and contained artifacts from nearby pre-Incan civilizations. The curator was very proud of this museum and so happy that we took an interest in it, that he invited us into the back where artifacts were identified and cataloged. He gave us information on the civilizations and restoration techniques and told us we would be allowed to handle the stone artifacts. Wanting to show an interest, I picked up an artifact, turned it in my hand as I studied it, and asked him what it was. He replied, "*Un falo*" (a phallus). I put it back on the table as quickly as I could. It was one of the most embarrassing moments of my life. I didn't ask any more questions.

It just so happened that the day we were in Samaipata was foundation day. (It was founded in 1618.) There was a huge celebration including a big soccer game with one of the neighboring villages and fireworks. The fireworks were mostly sparklers, pinwheels, and firecrackers which were attached to wooden frames carried by people moving through the crowd. Safety didn't seem to be a concern. There were hundreds of people present, and we were invited to join in the festivities. There were men walking through the crowd giving away glasses of *pisco* sour, and when the glass was empty, they would refill it.

Pisco sour is the national drink of Bolivia. It is made from Singani, lemon, sugar, and egg whites. Singani is a liquor distilled from grapes that grow in the region and has a high enough alcohol content to dissolve the pink painted label stenciled on the outside of the three liter Singani cans. After three or four *pisco* sours, I was celebrating along with the locals.

The intensity of the celebration was not slowing down, but we were, so we went back to the house, ate supper, and then spent much of the night talking and drinking wine. Sunday morning we went to the bus station and started our trip back to Santa Cruz. It was with a sense of sadness that we left Samaipata. It was such an enchanting and pleasant community. There are two things I recall about our trip back. One was the power line which was not one continuous strand, but a series of one or two hundred meter sections tied together. This must have gone on for fifty kilometers. The other, was a ten or twelve year old Bolivian girl singing along with a song coming over the bus's speaker system. It was Queen's "Another One Bites the Dust", but she was singing it "Another One Bites the Duts".

WALKING HOME FROM DOWNTOWN AT NIGHT

◦◦◦

On weekends, I spent most of my time downtown. I usually had errands to run or things to buy, and of course, socializing to do. If I happened to be out when it was near curfew, I would stay at the home of whichever teacher I was with. Sunday was different because with school the next day, I needed to be home the next morning. The buses stopped running at six o'clock, so if I was out after that, either by accident or design, I had to catch a taxi back home or walk.

The going rate for a taxi from downtown to the fourth ring was twenty pesos (one dollar), but there was a special *gringo* rate of fifty pesos. It didn't take me long to figure out that I needed to ask the price before I got into the taxi! About twenty percent of the time, I was quoted a fair price, and I rode the taxi home. I always gave a generous tip to reward the driver for not being a weasel and to encourage him for any future trips. The rest of the time I walked. It was not a bad walk at all, in fact it was quite enjoyable. I figured if I was unable to walk four kilometers, I shouldn't be out drinking.

About half the time, Larry or Al would be with me, which was nice because I would have company almost to the fourth ring. The rest of the time, I would walk home alone. There were street lights up to the third ring. Between the third and fourth rings, there was enough light from homes and businesses along the highway to see. At the second ring was the restaurant the *25 de Febrero* where we could stop if we were hungry. (I never knew the significance of that date.) The rest of the way the bars and *tiendas* were nicely spaced, out to the fourth ring.

The bars had tables and chairs, restrooms, *cacho* cups, and occasionally, snacks. We would sit down and enjoy a bottle of beer and play some *cacho*. Most of the bars had black and white TVs with either *novellas* (soap operas) or soccer games blaring away. At the fourth ring, I only had two blocks to go. When I reached the driveway where I lived, I would take out my keys and jingle them. This seemed to pacify my landlord's psycho dogs. One time they did try to attack me, and my landlord had to call them off. All in all, walking home from downtown at night was always an enjoyable pastime.

SHOOT ME IF YOU CAN

ᴄᴍ

One of the most terrifying experiences I had in Bolivia was the night a soldier tried to gun me down in the street like a dirty dog. It was the last Saturday before Lent and there was no curfew that night. Dan, Al, and I were downtown celebrating the night of the *mascaritas*.

The whole concept of *mascaritas* was odd, especially in such a male-dominated society like Bolivia. That one night women could do anything they wanted to (not kill anyone, but engage in any licentious behavior they wished, and have absolutely no consequences). Any woman could go into town that night, and her identity was protected by the mask she wore. This included married women! Their husbands did not object. Perhaps they wanted to, but the momentum of the custom prevented them from doing so. The mask was loose-fitting, like the hood given to a condemned man before he is hanged, so that a glass could be put up under the hood. There were holes cut out for the mouth and eyes. They were brightly colored: reds and oranges and pinks. There was one absolute rule: you NEVER unmasked a *mascarita*! If the woman chose to reveal herself to you that was her business. There were men who had sexual encounters with women and never knew their identity.

We were at one of the bars that had a large dance floor. It was quite crowded, and as I walked through a few of the women grabbed my ass (I was flattered). We spent most of the night dancing, and a little after three, we decided to walk home. After the second ring, the streets were deserted, so it was quiet. We walked past a guard station with a soldier asleep in a chair propped against the building. He had his hands on the rifle in his lap. To this day, I'm still not sure exactly what happened next. Evidently, our talking startled the guard. Al shouted, "Look out! He's got a gun!" Dan and Al took off running. The guard fired his rifle; the bullet passing so close to me, I could hear the bullet whiz past my head. My reflexes had been too slow: the guys were running down the sidewalk, the guard had the rifle pointed at my back, and I was walking away. I had the presence of mind to keep walking. I figured the guard would yell at me to halt or hit me over the head with the butt of his rifle, but he would not shoot me in the back (I didn't think he knew I was with the two running guys). I also knew if I stopped they could torture the truth out of me. I walked for a block and a half with his rifle trained on my back. At the corner, I turned right and when I was out of sight, I ran like hell! I spent about twenty minutes running down the back streets, hiding in the ditch whenever I heard a car coming. When I was a few blocks from the school, I saw the school van driving down the street. I jumped out and flagged it down. Larry was driving, and Dan and Al were with him. They had awakened Larry and told him I had been shot! I was so frightened that I was still shaking six hours later and could not go to sleep until that evening. It was fortunate that it was Sunday, because I was in no shape to be teaching.

The day was "water day". On this day virtually everyone in Santa Cruz threw water at everyone else. Squirt guns, water balloons, and hoses were the weapons of choice. The children targeted the police. I favored taxis with the windows rolled down. As we were in the backyard launching water balloons at a passers-by, the people next door turned the hose on us. The cool water felt refreshing in the hot, tropical sun. The next day was muddy water day. The day after that was "any liquid day" (except mineral acids and petroleum products). People would throw blood, paint, and urine among other things. The only people out on this day were hooligans. The following day was the first day of Lent. The Cruzeños needed forty days to return to normal!

THE PERFECT DAY

It was around seven in the morning when I was awakened by a loud chatter outside. A *surazo* had blown up from the south over night, so it was refreshingly cool in the cottage. I quickly dressed and went outside to see what all the racket was about. It was coming from the back of my landlord's property, where the cleared area for the orchard ended and the jungle began. I moved quietly, and as I reached the edge of the jungle, I saw a band of six or seven gray monkeys playing in the trees. A few minutes passed, and then one of the monkeys spied me and called out a warning. The band quickly disappeared into the jungle.

As I walked back to the house, I picked a papaya for breakfast. The papayas were so sweet, I usually had to put a few drops of lemon juice on them to cut the sweetness. There was a lemon in the refrigerator that I had picked the day before so I didn't have to pick a new one. As I ate breakfast, a cool breeze was blowing through the windows, and the radio was playing "Carry on My Wayward Son". Outside an occasional avocado would come crashing through the trees as it fell. The avocado trees were the size of oaks, and the dogs loved to eat the fallen fruit which were huge and very tasty.

After breakfast, I moved a chair outside to read in the warmth of the sun and listen to the radio. After an hour or so, I walked over to Sonya and Roxanne's for a beer. It was a beautiful day with a few clouds and flocks of parrots passing overhead. There were quite a few people on the fourth ring this morning, most walking or riding bicycles. Occasionally a family of four would ride by on a motorcycle. I was enjoying the tranquility of the moment when I noticed Al and Larry walking up the road. Funny how I always seemed to run into them at the *tienda*. We sat at a table under the big shade tree talking and playing *cacho*.

It must have been about noon when a couple of Brits showed up. They stopped by the *tienda* on occasion, so we were acquainted with them. We talked for a while, and they invited us over to their place for a cook out. We all walked over to their house which was about five blocks from the *tienda*. Over the next hour or so, around a dozen other people showed up, including two Irishmen who had spent the previous night sleeping outdoors without any mosquito netting. Their backs were covered with red welts from all the bites. I had never seen anyone so badly eaten up by mosquitoes.

There happened to be a vacant lot next door, so we decided to play some soccer. I played goalie because I didn't have the stamina to run around all the time. I actually did a decent job, making one spectacular save (by my reckoning) and a few mediocre ones. It was brutally hot in the sun, so we didn't play for long.

It was pleasantly cool inside the house even though they didn't have any air conditioning. We had a great meal which we nibbled at over the course of the afternoon. They had a toucan loose in the house, and it flew to the back of the couch where I was sitting. In an attempt to be friendly, I reached over to pet it, and it clacked its beak at me. I left it alone after that.

The party broke up around nine o'clock, and Dan and I walked back to the *tienda* to have a beer and play some *cacho*. I remember hearing some frogs with a weird call that sounded like a baby crying. After a couple hours, we made our way back home; it was clear, and we could see the Southern Cross in the sky. We stayed up talking and playing *cacho* for an hour or two then turned in. The memories of that day are so vivid that I can still relive it in it's entirety.

THE 220-VOLT SHOWER

⌒γ℘⌒

Not only can living in a developing country be trying, but it can be an adventure as well. Many things we take for granted in the United States, such as running water, electricity, or basic sanitation, do not exist, or exist in limited form. It is a brutal fact that in many parts of the world, extreme poverty makes these necessities into luxuries. These are luxuries that some governments cannot afford to provide for their people.

Public transportation was one area in which Bolivia was superior to the United States. I could ride a *micro* anywhere in Santa Cruz for a nickel. These small, clean buses held about twenty people, ran on a regular schedule, and were never overcrowded. When I felt more adventurous, I could ride a *colectivo*. These were the more traditional buses, that would be packed with pigs, people, and chickens until they were bursting out the windows and doors. *Colectivos* cost a penny to ride (unless you were hanging out the door, in which case you rode for free).

Many services were not as reliable as the buses. Periodically the power would go off for hours at a time for no apparent reason. If you didn't have a telephone, it took months to have one installed. If you did have one, you had to go all the way downtown to pay the bill in person. While you were downtown, you might as well go to the post office, because there was only one in the city, and there was no pick up or delivery of mail, except at the central post office. Teachers at Santa Cruz Cooperative School did not have to worry about this, because an employee of the school would drive into town each day to pick up the mail. Unfortunately, the average citizen of Santa Cruz did not enjoy this luxury.

There was one area in which we were singularly fortunate, and that was the Santa Cruz water system. Gulf Oil Corporation had supervised the design and installation of the water purification plant. This had been done so their employees would have a safe source of drinking water. As far as I know, Santa Cruz was the only city in Bolivia where a person could drink water out of the tap without first having to boil it.

I do not know how to discuss the next topic without seeming indelicate. It concerned the Santa Cruz sewage system. In Santa Cruz, you could not flush toilet paper down the commode! This was so important that the restrooms in the Santa Cruz International Airport had signs on the restroom walls warning against this dangerous practice. Used toilet paper had to be put into trash cans that sat next to the toilet. This disgusting practice had to be followed in homes as well as public restrooms. I found it astonishing that these trash cans were not the source of foul odors and flies. I was able to find out, after months of careful investigation, that the reason for this restriction was: 1.) the insides of the sewage pipes were not smoothed at the joints, so toilet paper would catch on the rough concrete sticking into the main flow of the pipe, or 2.) the sewage treatment plant did not have the capability to decompose toilet paper. In either case, I was extremely happy to return to the wonderful toilets in the USA.

Jim and Dave refused to follow this procedure in their home and used their toilet in a normal fashion. After a few months, their septic system clogged up, and they had to have the tank cleaned out. They described the procedure: two guys with shovels and plastic bags on their heads (to keep sewage out of their hair) jumped into the pit and shoveled it out. It cost them plenty. After that, they stopped putting paper in the toilet.

The most extraordinary fact of everyday life in Bolivia was that, with the exception of hotels and the homes of the very wealthy, there was no hot running water anywhere. Even in the tropics, bathing in cold water is uncomfortable. If you were taking a bath, you could heat water on the stove, but if you were taking a shower, you had to subject yourself to one of the most diabolical devices known to mankind: the 220-volt shower. The shower heads were all equipped with a built in heating coil. These were operated by a pressure switch which turned on the current to the coil when enough water flowed past the unit. The trick to taking a relaxing shower was to get the flow rate correct. If the water came out too fast, the coil couldn't heat the water fast enough, and it came out too cool. You could increase the temperature by slowing the flow rate, but if the rate was too slow, there would not be enough water pressure to activate the heater switch, and it would shut off giving you a blast of cold water. However, all this discussion of comfort is of minor importance when you consider safety. Just how safe is it to be standing in running water with a 220-volt electrical device centimeters above your head? I reached up once and felt a tingling sensation as my hand neared the shower head. One teacher, while rinsing her hair, accidentally touched the heating coil and was literally knocked out of the shower. I can picture the lady of the house walking out to greet her guests with her hair smoldering, "I just took a shower, and I can't do a thing with my hair."

DANCING WITH THE BROOM

⁓✱⁓

This chapter is a collection of experiences and observations of life in Santa Cruz in particular and the Bolivian culture in general. It is a series of vignettes illustrating some of the unusual and interesting aspects of living in a foreign country.

I had only been in Santa Cruz about a month when my landlord's daughter, Viqui, invited me to a party some of her friends were having. Most of the people at the party were my age, in their twenties or thirties, although I was the only *Norteamericano* present. I was sitting off to the side watching the couples dance when one of the young men approached me and handed me a broom. He could see the confused look on my face, so he took the broom, went out on the dance floor and began dancing with the broom. After a while, he approached a couple, gave the guy the broom, and began to dance with the girl. The displaced guy could find another girl to dance with, or go back to his original partner. Eventually, the broom wound up in my hands. I went out on the floor and danced with the broom until I found the prettiest girl on the floor, gave the broom to her partner, and danced with her for a while. I thought the broom was a nice way to meet people and involve everyone in the dancing.

The first few weeks in Santa Cruz, I rode the buses all over the city. It was an inexpensive way to tour the city and gave me the opportunity to get to know the surrounding area. Two of my favorite places were the zoo and the botanical gardens. The two things that made the biggest impression on me at the zoo were the large number of anteaters and a huge slide the length of a football field. It was at the botanical gardens that I saw one of the most beautiful sights ever: the blue morpho butterflies. Evidently they were attracted to the profusion of blossoms. They had a wingspan of ten to fifteen centimeters and were metallic blue with black trim on the wings.

One of the things that surprised me during my travels among the streets of Santa Cruz was the almost total absence of gas stations and traffic lights. I only saw four gas stations and maybe ten traffic lights in all of Santa Cruz. I saw more ox carts! The lack of traffic lights made driving interesting inside the first ring where two or three story buildings along the entire block made every corner a blind corner. All drivers, especially the taxi drivers, would barely slow down, honk their horns, and speed through the intersection. I was always afraid to ride a taxi inside the first ring. Once outside the third ring, there was less formality to the structure of the roads. Near our school there was a kapok tree growing in the middle of the sandy road. I don't know how long it had been growing there, but it was it was as tall as a three story building, and you couldn't put your arms around the base. People would just pass around it and didn't seem too concerned.

There were a wide variety of interesting birds in the tropics. The red birds and green parrots have already been mentioned. There were also birds which we were only able to identify by their call. The first was the "Star Wars" bird. It had a song that sounded like the weapons fired by the imperial storm troopers in the movie *Star Wars*. The other was the "Fuck You" bird. The name was onomatopoeic: that is what it sounded like the bird was saying when it would cry out. It was rare to see the spectacular multicolored birds, although I did see one once. Perhaps the most interesting birds were the weaver birds. Their football-sized nests were suspended from the tree branches which they wove from gathered grasses. These little yellow birds would enter the nests from a hole in the bottom and were always fun to watch.

Of all the people I met in Bolivia, two of them give some insight into the political climate of the country. Josecho owned a hamburger shop that served North American style hamburgers. I'd go there when I was getting homesick for the taste of the USA, and over the months, got to know him quite well. He had been trained in the States by McDonalds (which is why his burgers were so good). He was a middle class businessman in a country where only five percent of the population is middle class. He told me the local communists had approached him and instructed him not to oppose them when the revolution started (he didn't have to support them, just not oppose them). This was a time when the communists were actively expanding in Latin America so he took this advice seriously. The other person I knew was Klaus Altmann. I would see him playing cards with his cronies at the Shakespeare Bar. It was well known that he was a Nazi and had emigrated to Bolivia after the war like so many of his countrymen. He seemed pleasant enough, and I figured he had been some mid-level bureaucrat in the Nazi party during the war. It wasn't until about a year after I had returned to the States, that I heard on the news that he was actually Klaus Barbi, the Butcher of Lyon, and had been extradited to France to stand trial for war crimes! It is frightening to think that I could be that close to evil and not recognize it.

GOING HOME

I t was hard to believe the school year had passed so quickly, and it was time to return to the States. We started packing a week before we were due to fly out. Although I was homesick and anxious to go home, I already knew that I would miss Bolivia and the Bolivian people.

A lot had changed in my life since I first arrived in Bolivia. Most importantly, I was married. In fact, Linda and I were married twice: once in a civil ceremony in Spanish, and a second time in a church ceremony conducted in English. Larry's wife Joanne had done all the planning for the wedding reception, including decorating her house. She said it would be "the social event of the season". The teachers were all there, as well some of the American missionaries and oil people. Perhaps in the American community, it was the social event of the season.

Many of the missionaries had lived overseas for years and had raised their children in Bolivia. It surprised me that there were such a large number of expatriated Americans living in Bolivia. These were people who enjoyed the lifestyle and sense of freedom of living in a foreign country, in spite of the hardships. The junior high science teacher at SCCS had lived in Santa Cruz for seven years and had married a Bolivian woman. Another expat was John Dunston who owned the New Orleans Bar. (The New Orleans was located near the airport and catered to Americans.) A lot of the teachers and principals at SCCS had come from other overseas schools. Many of the Mennonites in the communities around Santa Cruz had made Bolivia their home, and over the years, their farms with trimmed shrubs and neatly cut lawns looked like dairy farms in Wisconsin. (They even put their metal milk cans out by the road to be picked up by the milk wagon!)

We had a lot of fun in Bolivia. The weirdest was the time eight or nine of us spent an hour in the Atomic Bar trying to name the seven dwarfs. One of the most memorable was the time one of the principals came back from the States with a turkey right before Thanksgiving. The teachers gathered at his house bringing potatoes, corn, cranberry sauce, and other dishes. We had a real American Thanksgiving, which even included a tape of a recent college football game which we watched. Sad to say, we lost track of most of our friends. The last time I heard from Larry, he was at a school in Brazil. Dan went to Central America and I lost track of him. Of all the teachers we knew in Bolivia, there are only two people we still keep in touch with.

Larry drove us to the airport and saw us off. As the airplane rose off the runway, I looked back at the city of Santa Cruz with a feeling of sadness. On the flight back to the States, we stopped at Manaus, Brazil for an hour or so and then continued on to Miami. As we went through customs, the customs official asked us what we were doing in Bolivia for a year, when we told him we were teachers, he just waved us through and said, "Welcome back to the United States."